The Ventnor West Branch Line

Peter A. Harding

Terrier 0-6-0T No.W.13 "Carisbrooke" taking water at Ventnor West Station. April 23rd 1949.
J.J.Smith

Published by
Peter A. Harding
"Mossgiel", Bagshot Road, Knaphill,
Woking, Surrey GU21 2SG.
ISBN 978 0 9552403 1 7

First published 1990. Revised edition 2007.
© Peter A. Harding 2007.
Printed by Binfield Print & Design Ltd.,
Binfield Road, Byfleet Village, Surrey KT14 7PN.

Contents

Introduction	3	Timetables & Tickets	25
History of the Line	4	Closure	26
Description of the Route	11	The Present Scene	29
Motive Power & Rolling Stock	21	Conclusion	31
Operation	24	Acknowledgements/Bibliography	32

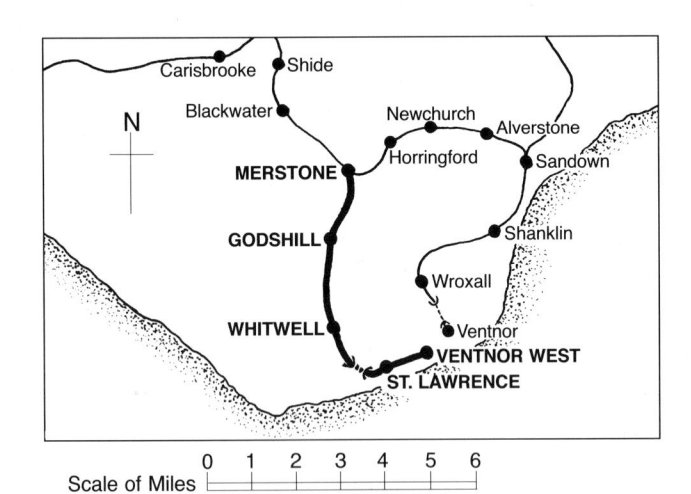

O2 class 0-4-4T No.W 30 "Shorwell" emerging from the St. Lawrence Tunnel with the branch train to Ventnor West. July 21st 1935.
S.W.Baker

Introduction

The Ventnor West branch line was the last railway to be built on the Isle of Wight and was opened from Merstone to St. Lawrence in 1897 and extended to Ventnor Town (later renamed Ventnor West) in 1900. It was considered by many to be not only the most picturesque railway on the Island but also on the whole of the south coast and offered passengers an enchanting journey with fine rural scenery between Merstone and the St. Lawrence Tunnel. On emerging from the tunnel, passengers were then treated to spectacular views out to sea followed by a run along the leafy Undercliff to Ventnor.

When originally opened there were high hopes of through traffic from the mainland via the Southampton and Cowes steam ferry service. Although some custom did come from this source and some through trains did in fact work from Cowes, it soon fell away in preference to the already established route from the mainland via the Portsmouth to Ryde steam ferry and then the Ryde Pier Head to Ventnor line which had been opened by the Isle of Wight Railway in 1866.

Apart from being the last line to be completed on the Island, the Ventnor West branch line also achieved the unfortunate record in 1952 of becoming the first line on the Island to close.

The picturesque approach to Ventnor West Station. September 13th 1952   J.J.Smith

History of the Line

During the early part of the 1800's, Ventnor, which at the time consisted of just a few small cottages and a watermill, was beginning to gain a reputation as a favourable recuperating place for people recovering from chest complaints. As more patients descended on the town, the population increased and more hospitals and convalescent homes including the Royal National Hospital for Diseases of the Chest and the Royal Hampshire County Hospital were built.

By the middle of the century the population was more than 3000 and with various proposals for railways on the Isle of Wight, Ventnor naturally hoped to be included.

The first proposal involving Ventnor was for a line from Cowes via Newport with a branch from Newport to Ryde. Next came the Ryde & Ventnor Railway followed by a scheme which became known as "The Corkscrew Line" because it would have run from Ventnor to Sandown then across to Newport via Ashey and Mersley Down with branches to Ryde and Cowes. None of these schemes came to fruition but a line linking Cowes and Newport was sanctioned. Known as the Cowes & Newport Railway it opened on June 16th 1862, becoming the first line to be built on the Island.

The second line to be built did in fact include Ventnor and was built by the Isle of Wight Railway who were incorporated as the Isle of Wight (Eastern Section) Railway to build a line from Ryde to Ventnor via Brading, Sandown and Shanklin. The 'Eastern Section' was later dropped from the title.

This line was opened from Ryde to Shanklin on August 23rd 1864, but due to unforeseen delays involving construction of a tunnel under St. Boniface Down the section from Shanklin to Ventnor via Wroxall was not opened until September 10th 1866. The station at Ventnor was built at the end of the tunnel from St. Boniface Down in an old quarry which was situated high above the town.

After some years, a growing discontent towards the Isle of Wight Railway by the people of Ventnor plus the situation of the station led to suggestions of perhaps an alternative line to the town with a more accessible station.

In 1871 the Yarmouth & Ventnor Railway, Tramway & Pier Company was proposed which would have run from Yarmouth to Ventnor via Freshwater Bay and Chale, but this scheme was later abandoned.

In 1886 the Shanklin & Chale Railway was authorised to build a line between these two places and then west to Freshwater. Having failed to raise sufficient capital, plans were abandoned in 1889 in favour of an entirely new plan which was put forward for a line to run from what would be a junction at Merstone on the Isle of Wight Central Railway to terminate beyond a tunnel at St. Lawrence via Godshill and Whitwell. This proposal received its Act on August 12th 1889 as the Newport, Godshill & St. Lawrence Railway with a capital of £112,000. In 1892 a further Act was received authorising an extension from St. Lawrence along an area known as the Undercliff to terminate at Steephill Castle on the outskirts of Ventnor. This new line to Ventnor would give passengers a more direct route from Cowes with its steam ferry connections to Southampton and would hopefully open up new traffic from the mainland.

The engineer appointed by the Newport, Godshill & St. Lawrence Railway was Mr.R.Elliott Cooper who held a distinguished position in his profession and had worked in other parts of the world. The company secretary was Mr.John Scowen and the solicitor was Mr.W.Bohn who was later to become the company chairman. The contractors appointed to build the line were Messrs. Westwood & Winby, and, under a special agreement, the line was to be worked by the Isle of Wight Central Railway.

The first sod of the new railway was turned at Merstone on Tuesday April 19th 1893 by Miss Beatrice Kate Martin, a niece of Mr.Henry Martin who was affectionately dubbed the 'father' of the Islands railways by way of his association with the very first line to be built on the Island, the Cowes & Newport Railway.

The proceedings attracted a large and influential gathering with most parts of the Island being represented. The station at Merstone and the immediate neighbourhood was decorated with bunting. The *Isle of Wight County Press* reported the event in their Saturday April 22nd 1893 edition in the following delightful manner:- *(Note the original spelling 'Merston '.)*

"Very gracefully and expertly did Miss Martin perform the task allotted to her. With a mahogany-handled, silver-bladed spade she turned the first sod - several sods in fact - placing them in a mahogany, silver-mounted barrow, and then wheeling them along a plank to their appointed destination, and returning with the barrow along the same narrow way without once "running off the line" - a feat which the spectators loudly cheered. The blade of the spade bore the following inscription: "Presented by Messrs. Westwood and Winby to Miss Beatrice Kate Martin on the occasion of her cutting the first sod of the Newport, Godshill and St. Lawrence Railway. Merston, April 19th 1893." On a silver plate at the back of the barrow was Miss Martin's monogram, with the name of the railway and the date of the ceremony. The spade and barrow, which were very handsome, were supplied by Messrs. Mappin Brothers, of London."

During the construction of the line, the contractors Westwood & Winby were declared bankrupt in July 1895 and work was held up until the following November when Mr. Charles Westwood reformed the company in the name of C.J. Westwood & Co.

Three engines were known to be employed during the construction, one, which was a 2-4-0 well tank was formerly used in the construction of the Bembridge branch where it was called "St. Helens". In September 1893 it was bought by Charles Westwood for £650 from the Brading Harbour Improvement & Railway Company (who built the Bembridge branch) and renamed "St. Lawrence". In May 1897 a small 0-6-0 saddle tank which was built by the Worcester Engineering Company in 1863 and later rebuilt by Kerr, Stuart & Co. in 1895 (and worked their Stoke-on-Trent works as "California") was obtained and renamed "Godshill". The third engine was called "Weaste" and was a small 0-4-0 saddle tank which had been built by Hudswell Clarke in 1888 for the contractor T.A.Walker while he was constructing the Manchester Ship Canal.

The line was opened from Merstone to St. Lawrence for a special "press" run on Saturday July 17th 1897. On Monday July 19th a more formal and elaborate inauguration took place and on Tuesday July 20th the line was opened for public traffic. For the "press" inspection on the Saturday, a number of representatives from the Island and mainland journals attended in response to an invitation from Mr.Charles L.Conacher the manager of the Isle of Wight Central Railway (by whom the line was to be worked) and also from Mr. Charles Westwood representing the contractors. The *Isle of Wight County Press* reported in their Saturday July 24th 1897 edition as follows:-

"The party had the happiness to be "personally conducted" by Mr.Conacher, and a model "personal conductor" he proved himself to be. On arriving at Merston Junction the visitors were met by Mr.Charles Westwood, Mr.Wynter (contractors's engineer), Mr.Knights (assistant engineer), and other officials, and after making an inspection of the important-looking junction, with its spacious platforms, the party were conveyed by special train over the new line, stopping at the stations, the tunnel, and other points of interest *en route*. There were many features arresting attention, amongst these being the excellence which marks the construction of the line throughout, the smoothness of running, the high-class appearance of the stations, the amplitude of the platforms spaces, especially at Merston, Godshill, and Whitwell, the commodiousness of the station-masters' houses, the extensiveness of the provision made for goods traffic, and the admirable completeness with which all the essential details of a thoroughly efficient railway service have been carried out. And then the natural scenes! The line passes through a most picturesque part of the Island, landscapes of exquisite rural beauty being offered at every turn to the admiring eye, and, as a crowning spectacle, just as St. Lawrence is reached a glorious view of the sea burst upon the enraptured sight – "Pictures for Memory to ponder over," as the Poet of the "Fair Island" says in his description of this charming part of the Wight. Although St. Lawrence – Ventnor St. Lawrence, if you please – is the present terminus, the line is to be continued to the Capital of the Undercliff, and indeed, the work is already in progress. Meanwhile, convenient facilities will be afforded at St. Lawrence for the conveyance of passengers from that place to Ventnor. The station here will be on the low level, and this will be voted a precious public boon. Oh, that toilsome ascent from Ventnor to the existing railway station! It is on record that experienced Alpine travellers have paled before that awful steep, and it has been further suggested that Shakespeare must have had a prevision of it when he wrote of a "climbing sorrow" and bade it avaunt! Be this as it may, the character of a public benefaction is claimed for an undertaking which enables railway passengers to and from Ventnor to escape that bit of mountaineering."

The inaugural ceremonials took place on the following Monday (July 19th) and was attended by a large and influential group of people, both from the Island and the mainland. In fact, a special saloon carriage was attached to the 9.15 a.m. train from Waterloo to accommodate the special guests. The party arrived at Ryde Pier Head shortly before 1.00 p.m. from where they went by a special train with saloon carriages and a gaily decorated Isle of Wight Central Railway engine (No.6, a 4-4-0 tank built by Black Hawthorn) which for the occasion had a screen on the buffer beams announcing "Success to the Newport, Godshill & St. Lawrence Railway". Mr.Charles L.Conacher was in charge and gave the guests a hearty welcome.

The ceremonial first train on July 19th 1897, pulled by the Isle of Wight Central Railway 4-4-0 engine No.6. The fireman in the cab is Mr.F.Young and standing next to the engine are (left to right) Messrs.J.Seymour (Locomotive Superintendent), C.L.Conacher (General Manager), J.Pierce (Driver), S.Lovett (Clerk), W.Matthews (Guard) and W.Bell (Carriage Examiner). Lens of Sutton

At 1.40 p.m. the train steamed into St. Lawrence Station (which was of course the temporary terminus) where it was greeted with bunting, sounds of fog-signals and cheers from spectators. After the guests alighted, the train shunted back towards the St. Lawrence Tunnel while the party of guests moved to the west end of the platform where an important ceremony took place. Conducted by Mr. Westwood, Mr.Wynter and Mr. Knights (for the contractors), Mrs.Percy Mortimer (wife of Percy Mortimer a director of not only the Newport, Godshill & St. Lawrence Railway but also the Isle of Wight Central Railway) armed with a brand new and specially made spanner which was decorated with red, white and blue ribbons proceeded to screw up the last bolt in one of the fish plates of the permanent way which had purposely been left for the occasion. When this task was completed, the train passed over the joint which was declared secure. After more cheers from the spectators, the whole party proceeded to nearby Elm Dene, the residence of Mr.& Mrs.Charles Westwood where an elegant luncheon was served in a spacious marquee which had been erected in the grounds.

Many enthusiastic speeches were made, all basking in the glory of the new railway, the most noticeable coming from the following:-

Mr.T.D.Bolton, M.P. (Chairman of the Isle of Wight Central Railway) who presided over the proceedings made the following interesting statement:- "It was his honest belief that the Isle of Wight owed its prosperity to the railways and to nothing else. Might they flourish root and branch till time and memory be no more". He went on to say that he believed the new line would be as successful as any in the Isle of Wight.

General the Hon.Somerset J.G.Calthorpe, J.P., C.A. (Chairman of the Isle of Wight County Council) said "a smoother and a better line he had never ridden over".

Mr.Percy Mortimer proposed the health of the contractors Messrs.C.J. Westwood & Co. saying what a difficult job they had in finding the cash and also other difficulties to contend with which were not anticipated, yet, they had built a really first class line.

Just as Mr. Westwood rose to respond, a group of his navvies swooped down into the garden singing "For he's a jolly good fellow". This interruption created great amusement. Mr. Westwood said a contractor's lot was not a happy one, especially on such a work as he had just carried out, but after all he was still in love with his profession and was proud to see the line opened that day as far as St. Lawrence. He thanked Mr.Bolton and the General for their kind remarks about the line and he felt perfectly convinced in his own mind that eventually, under the able management of Mr.Conacher, to whom he was very thankful for much kind assistance, the new line would be the best paying railway in the Isle of Wight. Mr.Westwood went on to say (to the amusement of the gathering) that he regretted that he could not make speeches but, as the navvy said, he could shift muck.

In concluding the speeches, Mr.T.D.Bolton then addressed himself to the probable prospects of the new line. He believed that this railway was going to be a great success, but success could only be assured when they extended the line along the Undercliff to Steephill Castle at Ventnor. At this point, Mr.Westwood proudly added "We shall be there in six months".

The following day (Tuesday July 20th), the line was opened for traffic and many local residents made their first journey over the new railway. As the company had still to complete the remaining section to Ventnor, an arrangement was made with Mr.F.Baker jr., of 25, Pier Street, Ventnor to run a horse coach service between St. Lawrence Station and Ventnor where a ticket office was opened at 22, Pier Street, the fare being fixed at 6d.

Although Charles Westwood had boldly announced that having reached St. Lawrence, Ventnor would be reached in six months time, he was soon to run into further financial trouble and by the turn of the year was bankrupt once again and unable to complete the section along the Undercliff to Ventnor. Another contractor had to be found and after some while, J.T.Firbank, a well known contractor in the south of England accepted the job and made use of the plant which Charles Westwood had left behind.

A group of the navvies involved in the construction of the St. Lawrence to Ventnor extension, pose for this photograph with the 0-6-0 saddle tank "Godshill". The location is thought to be just to the east of St. Lawrence Station.
Author's Collection

The building of the extension did not prove so easy as was at first thought, the route having to pass through the Steephill Castle estate and, it was this estate which caused all the problems. After prolonged negotiation, Mr.Charles Mortimer, brother of director Percy Mortimer, bought the whole estate and disposed of the land to the Newport, Godshill & St. Lawrence Railway at a reasonable price.

The extension was finally opened to the public on Friday, June 1st 1900. The *Isle of Wight County Press* reported the event in their Saturday June 9th 1900 edition as follows:- *(Note how the company are described as the Ventnor, Godshill and Newport Railway)*

THE COWES AND VENTNOR DIRECT
OPENING OF THE NEW LINE

As reported in our issue of last Saturday the opening of the new direct railway route to Ventnor was successfully accomplished on the previous day, when the Chairman and some of the Directors of the Ventnor, Godshill and Newport Railway together with the Chairman and Manager of the I.W.Central Railway and a number of Press representatives (including a lady), and several friends came from London to attend the interesting proceedings. They travelled *via* Southampton and Cowes and arrived in Ventnor a few minutes before two o'clock. After the inspection of the extension of the line from St. Lawrence through the lovely Undercliff scenes to Ventnor Town station, with which every one was apparently pleased, an adjournment was made to the Royal Hotel, at the invitation of the Chairman of the Company, where a sumptuous *dejeune* was served.

The chair was taken by Mr.W.Bohm, the chairman of the new line, who was supported on his right by Mr.T.D.Bolton, M.P. (Chairman of the I.W.Central Railway), Mr.Percy Mortimer, Mr.G.B.Purkis (Mayor of Newport), Dr.Robertson (Chairman of the Ventnor District Council), Capt.Dunstan and Mr.H.Magnus, joint directors of the new line and the Central Railway, Mr.J.C.Inglis (engineer of the Great Western Railway), Mr.Percy Dunstan (secretary of the Ventnor, Newport and Godshill Line), Mr.R.Elliott Cooper (engineer of the new line), Mr.C.L.Conacher (general manager of the Central and of the new line), Capt.Lloyd, and representatives of the London and local Press. Mr.Conacher was in the vice-chair.

After speeches from first the Chairman Mr.W.Bohm, followed by Dr.Robertson, Mr.Charles Mortimer and Mr.G.B.Purkis. Mr.J.C.Inglis had the following to say:-

"The view when the train emerged from the tunnel at St. Lawrence, he was quite satisfied, could not be surpassed, and he knew Devonshire and Cornwall and many other parts of England well - it was a more impressive scene than any he remembered (applause). In the soil and the configuration of the ground they had other advantages - the Island combined what was somewhat rare, an excellent climate and a fruitful soil (applause). None who had journeyed with them could have failed to admire the scenery through which the extension of the new line passed, and he believed that with all those advantages there was a great future for the Undercliff (hear, hear). As time went on and they all became busier and busier, the question of saving fifteen minutes in the journey there was a very important element. He was associated with the Great Western Railway Company, and to some extent likewise with the Midland and South Western Railways. They wished this line to Ventnor every success, and they hoped to send many passengers to visit that lovely neighbourhood (loud applause)".

Isle of Wight Central Railway 2-4-0T No.5 pulls a train of 4-wheeled stock towards Ventnor Town in 1901, soon after the opening of the extension. R.Stumpf Collection

Although the Newport, Godshill & St. Lawrence Railway had high hopes of through traffic from not only Newport and Cowes but also the mainland via Cowes, it is interesting to note that in their minutes recorded in 1895, the Company Seal of Approval should be given to the proposed Ashey & Horringford Junction Railway which, if built, would have linked Ashey on the Ryde to Newport line and Horringford on the Newport to Sandown line and, by providing a triangular junction at Merstone would give the new line to Ventnor two options of through traffic from the mainland and a distinct advantage over the Isle of Wight Railway station at Ventnor by tapping some of their custom.

Unfortunately for the Newport, Godshill & St. Lawrence Railway, capital for the proposed Ashey to Horringford line was not forthcoming and the scheme was dropped.

As previously mentioned, the new line to Ventnor was worked from the outset by the Isle of Wight Central Railway and after many financial problems it came as no great surprise that on April 8th 1913 the Newport, Godshill & St. Lawrence Railway ceased to exist and was absorbed by the Isle of Wight Central Railway.

Gradient Profile

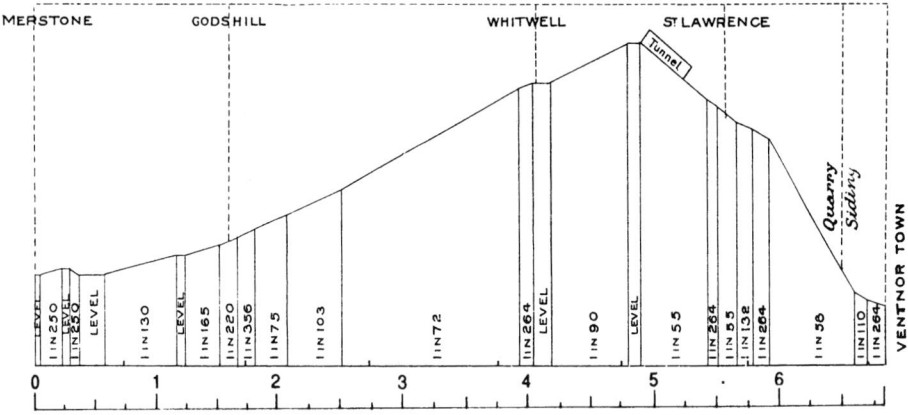

After the 1923 grouping, all the Island's railways passed into the hands of the Southern Railway who, having inherited two stations at Ventnor decided to take the logical step and rename the former Newport, Godshill & St. Lawrence Railway Ventnor Town Station to the more realistic title of Ventnor West.

Nationalisation took place in 1948 and the Southern Railway became British Railways Southern Region and, although the line to Ventnor West ran through scenery which was generally acknowledged as unrivalled for its beauty anywhere on the south coast, the fact remained that public use of the line had progressively dwindled over a period of years.

Despite many protests, the line closed completely on and from September 15th 1952.

Isle of Wight Central Railway 2-4-0T No.5 with 4-wheeled stock at Ventnor Town Station in 1901.

Author's Collection

Description of the Route

The station at Merstone was opened when the 4¾ mile section between Horringford and Shide was brought into action by the then Isle of Wight (Newport Junction) Railway on February 1st 1875 as part of their line to connect Newport and Sandown. Originally, the station had a single platform but when the Newport, Godshill & St. Lawrence Railway was opened in 1897, the station was upgraded to a junction, and was rebuilt into a 301 ft. island platform by the Isle of Wight Central Railway (who had been formed in July 1887 when the Cowes & Newport Railway, the Ryde & Newport Railway and the Isle of Wight (Newport Junction) Railway amalgamated).

A pedestrian underpass was also built so that passengers could reach the island platform without crossing over the line, which must have been quite a luxury for such a small village. Unfortunately, the underpass often flooded during wet weather as a nearby small brook which flowed under the railway often overspilled. The Southern Railway later filled in the underpass and replaced it with a pedestrian access ramp.

MERSTONE STATION

O2 class 0-4-4T No. W 36 "Carisbrooke" waits at the branch platform at Merstone ready for a run to Ventnor West.
Lens of Sutton

Two views taken from the signal box at Merstone. *(Left)* Looking towards the station, *(right)* looking towards the junction with the line to Ventnor West branching off to the right.
John Grant

Early timetables described trains as 'down' to Ventnor and 'up' to Merstone (see 1909 timetable on page 25). Later, the Isle of Wight Central Railway followed by the Southern Railway revised this policy stating that trains to Ventnor were 'up' and vice-versa. However, for this publication the direction will be described as the original timetables i.e. 'down' to Ventnor and 'up' to Merstone.

An early view of Merstone Station showing the pedestrian underpass before the Southern Railway later filled it in.
Author's Collection

Trains for Ventnor Town (later West) would normally leave Merstone from the newer loop platform, passing the large signal box and crossing the road on the level, before curving off to the right from the Sandown route and heading south over a rather remote part of the island first climbing at a gradient of 1 in 250 then dropping 1 in 250 before climbing 1 in 130, then 1 in 165 followed by 1 in 220 to reach Godshill.

The pull-and-push train from Ventnor West (right) approaches Merstone while the Sandown to Newport train (left) waits for the signal. The Merstone signal box was the only one on the island which controlled the level crossing gates by a wheel. June 28th 1950.
Pamlin Prints

12

The station at Godshill was 1 mile 48 chains from Merstone and appeared to be out in the middle of some fields about half a mile from the village. There was a substantial two-storey brick built station house and a single-storey station building (containing ticket office and waiting room) joined to it on a 300 ft. single platform. The platform was on the 'down' (east) side of the single line and was completed by a 260 ft. long goods siding which ran in behind the platform from the south end of the line. In 1928, the station was downgraded to an unstaffed halt.

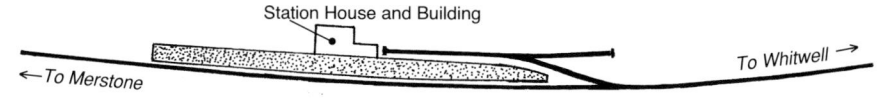

GODSHILL STATION

Godshill Station looking towards Merstone. The goods siding is behind the platform. Lens of Sutton

Another view of Godshill Station, this time looking towards Whitwell. Lens of Sutton

13

On leaving Godshill, the line continued its climb up a gradient of 1 in 220, 1 in 356, 1 in 75, 1 in 103, 1 in 72 and 1 in 264 before reaching the station at Whitwell which was 4 miles 2 chains from Merstone. When the branch first opened, Whitwell Station had a passing loop with two platforms and a signal box which controlled the points to a 360 ft. long siding. The 'down' platform (east side of the line) was 258 ft. long and housed the two-storey station house which was very similar to that at Godshill and, like Godshill, it also had a single-storey station building (containing the ticket office and waiting room) joined to it, while the 258 ft. long 'up' platform (west side of the line) had just a small waiting shelter.

After the Southern Railway took over in 1923 it soon became obvious that the small amount of traffic could not justify the expense of a crossing loop, so, in 1926 it was taken out of use. The signal box was also removed in the late 1920's. Like Godshill, Whitwell was also unstaffed in 1928, although it was sometimes staffed during the summer months and did not officially become a halt until 1941.

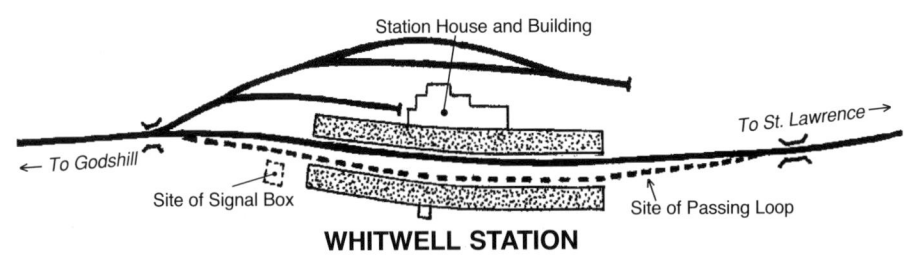

WHITWELL STATION

Looking towards Godshill from Whitwell Station before the passing loop and signal box were removed. H.C.Casserley

Looking towards St. Lawrence from Whitwell Station at a similar time. Lens of Sutton

Another view of the original station layout at Whitwell looking towards St. Lawrence soon after the line had opened showing the sidings, passing loop and the signal box. Lens of Sutton

A later view at Whitwell with the passing loop and the signal box removed. Lens of Sutton

Taken at the same time at Whitwell but looking the other way towards Godshill. Lens of Sutton

15

From Whitwell the line climbed at a gradient of 1 in 90 for about three quarters of a mile before passing over the Whitwell-Ventnor B3327 road by a level crossing. This crossing was known as Dean Crossing and was the only level crossing on the branch apart from the one at Merstone Junction. Surprisingly, a pedestrian footbridge was also provided here for anyone who might be delayed at the crossing gates.

O2 class 0-4-4T No.W 27 "Merstone" passing over Dean Crossing with the last train from Merstone to Ventnor West on September 13th 1952.
Pamlin Prints

The well appointed setup at Dean Crossing showing the substantial crossing keeper's house and footbridge, looking south towards St. Lawrence.
Author's Collection

From Dean Crossing the line went into a cutting through the downs and then entered the St. Lawrence Tunnel (also known as High Hat Tunnel) which was 619 yards long. In the tunnel, the gradient dropped to 1 in 55 before the line emerged at the south end on a 14 chain left hand curve where passengers were treated to magnificent panoramic views along the coast as the line headed towards St. Lawrence Station.

The south portal of St. Lawrence Tunnel .   Author's Collection

Terrier 0-6-0T No.W 8 "Freshwater" with a pull-and-push set heads from the tunnel down the bank towards St. Lawrence. October 10th 1934.   S.W.Baker

17

Terrier 0-6-0T No.W 8 "Freshwater" with pull-and-push set No.484 coasting along the Undercliff towards St. Lawrence heading for Ventnor West. July 23rd 1935. S.W.Baker

    St. Lawrence Station was 5 miles 44 chains from Merstone and its single 220 ft. platform which stood on the 'up' (south) side of the line was located on a 1 in 55 down gradient. The station building here was like Godshill and Whitwell inasmuch as it was a two-storey brick building but was different by being an all-in one house and station building without a canopy. St. Lawrence was the most southerly station on the Island and appeared to be squashed between the downs and a public road which crossed over the line by an adjoining road bridge. At one time a short siding existed just beyond the road bridge but was later removed. Like Godshill (and later Whitwell), St. Lawrence was also reduced to an unstaffed halt in 1927.

The station at St. Lawrence which by now was an unstaffed halt looking towards Ventnor West. September 13th 1952. J.J.Smith

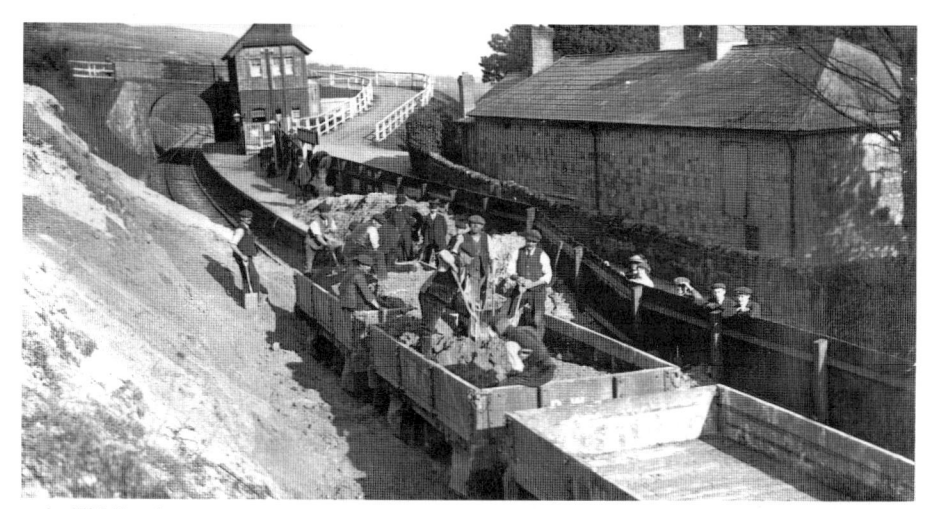

A cliff fall at St. Lawrence after wet weather in 1903. The short siding which lasted for the first few years after the line opened, can just be seen beyond the bridge. Lens of Sutton

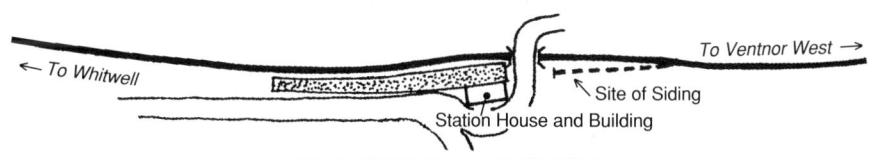

ST. LAWRENCE STATION

← To Whitwell   To Ventnor West →
Site of Siding
Station House and Building

The platform at St. Lawrence looking towards the tunnel and Whitwell. Lens of Sutton

19

On leaving St. Lawrence Station, the line continued on a steady down gradient ranging from 1 in 55, 1 in 132, 1 in 264 and 1 in 58 along the pleasant route towards Ventnor. For some years, a quarry siding existed on the north side of the line before Ventnor was reached on a down gradient of 1 in 110 and 1 in 264. Ventnor West Station was 6 miles 68 chains from Merstone and as previously mentioned was originally called Ventnor Town, but, when the Southern Railway took over the Islands railways they renamed it Ventnor West. The station consisted of two 337 ft platforms, although the 'down' (north) platform was rarely used as most trains would arrive at the 'up' (south) platform ready for the return journey. This platform also contained the two-storey station house and single-storey station building but, unlike the brick buildings at the other stations on the branch, this building was of a more substantial grey stone.

On approaching the station, a 360 ft. long goods siding branched off to the north of the line and in turn this siding forked with a goods shed at the end of the more northerly of the two, while the 480 ft. coal siding finished behind the 'down' platform. A short 60 ft. siding complete with an inspection pit next to a water tank and column branched off to the south of the line on the approach to the station. One striking feature on arriving at Ventnor West was the tall signal box which was located on the approach to the 'down' platform.

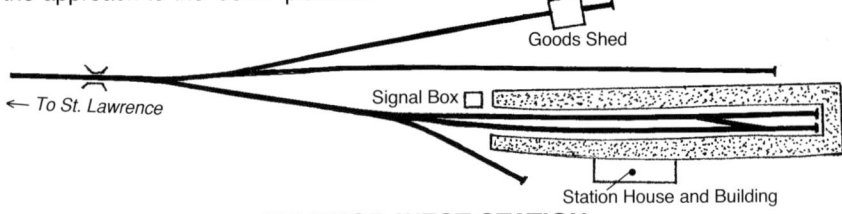

VENTNOR WEST STATION

Ventnor West Station looking towards the buffer stops. The station nameboard proudly states that the station is 168 ft above sea level.

Lens of Sutton

Motive Power and Rolling Stock

As mentioned previously, the branch was worked from the outset by the Isle of Wight Central Railway and, although the Black Hawthorn 4-4-0T No.6 was the locomotive which pulled the opening train on July 19th 1897, the passenger service was first worked by "Godshill" the small 0-6-0 saddle tank on hire from the contractors and later by "Sandown", a Beyer Peacock 2-4-0T on loan from the Isle of Wight Railway.

In May 1898, the Isle of Wight Central Railway took delivery of a Beyer Peacock 2-4-0T which became their No.8 and this locomotive soon proved a great success on the branch.

During the early part of the century, many of the mainland railway companies were using steam or petrol driven railcars on branch lines and other short distance passenger services. With this in mind the Isle of Wight Central Railway (with some advice from the mainland) decided to obtain a steam railcar for use on the branch. The engine portion was built by R. & W. Hawthorn & Co. while the carriage portion was built by Hurst Nelson & Co. and cost £1,450 plus delivery charge. It reached the Island in October 1906 where it became Steam Railcar No.1 and was capable of carrying 50 passengers. It soon entered regular service on the branch and greatly impressed the Isle of Wight Central Railway board.

With the success of Steam Railcar No.1, the board decided to obtain another slightly larger version, but on receiving a quotation of £2,040 for a 65 seater with one third more power, it was decided that this price was too high and that the Black Hawthorn 0-4-2 engine No.3 (originally called "Mill Hill") would be rebuilt by encasing the boiler and footplate and by fitting mechanical pull-and-push gear. This was close coupled to a composite bogie carrige which was purchased from the Midland Railway for £250 to form a type of 'home made' steam railcar. .

Unfortunately, this vehicle proved a disappointment and the former Midland Railway carriage was converted back for normal service while the engine, with casing removed, returned to shunting duties at the Medina Wharf.

Isle of Wight Central Railway 2-4-0T No.5 returning from Ventnor Town along the Undercliff between Ventnor and St. Lawrence. R.Stumpf Collection

Before the original conversion took place, the former Midland Railway carriage briefly worked the branch with one of the four former London Brighton & South Coast Railway Stroudley "Terrier" 0-6-0T's (which the Isle of Wight Central Railway had purchased between 1899 and 1903) whenever Steam Railcar No.1 was unavailable.

In 1908, Steam Railcar No.1 was transferred to the Freshwater branch and the line was then worked by a "Terrier" with a set of 4-wheel carriages until April 1925 when the Southern Railway (who absorbed all the Island's railways at the 1923 grouping) brought over from the mainland some motor train equipped Adams O2 class 0-4-4T's which they had inherited from the London South Western Railway.

These O2's were considered excessive for the branch and were soon switched to the former Isle of Wight Railway line from Ryde Pier Head to Ventnor, while some of the" Terriers" were fitted with the necessary train-control equipment and worked the branch until only three remained on the Island (one of these three returned to the mainland in 1947 and the other two in 1949). From 1949, the Adams O2's returned to take over branch duties until the line closed in 1952.

Isle of Wight Central Railway Steam Railcar No.1.　　　　　R.Stumpf Collection

Isle of Wight Central Railway engine No.3 coupled to the former Midland Railway bogie carriage to form the 'home made' steam railcar on the Undercliff.　　　　　Author's Collection

The Isle of Wight Central Railway had a great variety of carriages at the time the branch opened, mostly 4-wheelers which had been brought over from the mainland and many of these 4-wheelers were seen on the branch from the opening.

In the early 1920's, former London, Chatham & Dover Railway 4-wheel pull-and-push stock arrived for service. Originally built as 6-wheelers, they were converted to 4-wheelers at the same time that they were being converted to pull-and-push.

Later, former London Brighton & South Coast Railway stock was used until the branch closed. On many occasions, just a single former London Brighton & South Coast Railway composite coach (No. 6987) was used with a locomotive.

Terrier 0-6-0T No.W 8 "Freshwater" with a former London, Chatham & Dover Railway pull-and-push set at Godshill. April 13th 1936.
S.W.Baker

Former London, Brighton and South Coast Railway pull-and-push set No.503 with O2 class 0-4-4T No. W 35 "Freshwater" at Ventnor West Station. July 28th 1951.
Pamlin Prints

Operation

When first opened, the line from Merstone to Ventnor was worked by Preece's staff and ticket system with a passing loop and block post at Whitwell, but, after the Southern Railway had taken over, the loop and signal box at Whitwell were taken out of use and later removed and the whole section from Merstone to Ventnor was worked as a one engine in steam branch.

Having made this economy and then introducing pull-and-push trains, the Southern Railway then introduced conductor/guards which meant that the guards sold tickets on the trains and that booking offices at Godshill, Whitwell and St. Lawrence were then closed, although Whitwell was sometimes staffed during the summer. Ventnor West was staffed throughout

A general view of Ventnor West Station from the buffer stops. June 28th 1950. *Denis Cullum*

Isle of Wight Central Railway 0-4-4T No.2 (formerly of the Marquess of Londonderry's Railway) on a very rare occasion that this heavy engine worked the Ventnor Town branch. Seen here approaching St. Lawrence with some 4-wheeled stock soon after the line had opened. *L.C.G.B. Ken Nunn Collection*

Timetables and Tickets

OCTOBER 1909

DOWN. WEEK-DAYS. SUNDAYS.

			1	2	3	4	5	6	7	8	9	1	2
Miles			Goods a.m.	Mixed a.m.	Pass. a.m.	Pass. noon	Pass. p.m.	Exprs p.m.	Pass p.m.	Mixed p.m.	Pass. p.m.	Mixed a.m.	Pass p.m.
	MERSTONE Jct.	dep	7 0	9 18	10 32	12 10	1 20	pass	5 35	8 15		9 24	9 30	8 34
1½	Godshill A	dep	7 15	9 22	10 36	12 13	1 25	4 4	5 39	8 19		9 28	9 35	8 39
4	Whitwell	,,	7 45	9 29	10 41	12 18	1 31	4 A9	5 45	8 24		9 33	9 40	8 45
5¼	St. Lawrence A	,,	7 55	9 35	10 45	12 22	1 35	4 A12	5 50	8 31		9 37	9 45	8 50
6¼	VENTNOR Town	arr	8 5	9 40	10 50	12 25	1 40	4 15	5 55	8 35		9 40	9 50	8 55

A. Stops by Signal.
N.B. All Passenger Trains must stop momentarily outside Ventnor Home Signals - Goods Trains to stop dead.
NOTES. Week-days
No. 1 Take all Ventnor Line Wagons Must work to time. Shunt Ventnor Yard o arrival. Load Sand when required. No. 3, 4, 6 & 8 Through Trains Cowes to Ventnor Town
ELECTRIC BLOCK Merstone Junction, Godshill, Whitwell, Ventnor Town
TELEPHONE. Same, including St. Lawrence.

UP. WEEK-DAYS. SUNDAYS

			1	2	3	4	5	6	7	8	9	1	2
Miles			Mixed a.m.	Pass. a.m.	Pass. a.m.	Pass noon	Mixed p.m.	Pass. p.m.	Pass p.m.	Pass p.m.	Pass p.m.	Mixed a.m.	Pass p.m.
	VENTNOR Town	dep	8 25	9 45	10 55	12 30	1 35	4 45	6 0	8 40		9 45	10 35	9 0
1¼	St. Lawrence A		8 30	9 50	10 59	12 34	1 39	4 49	6 4	8 44		9 49	10 39	9 4
2¼	Whitwell	dep	8 35	9 55	11 3	12 38	2 43	4 53	6 8	8 48		9 53	10 44	9 8
5¼	Godshill A		8 40	9 59	11 7	12 42	2 47	4 57	6 12	8 52		9 57	10 48	9 12
6¼	MERSTONE Jct.	arr	8 45	10 2	11 10	12 46	2 50	4 59	6 15	8 55		10 0	10 52	9 16

NOTES. —Week-days. A Calls by Signal.
No. 1 to bring all Ventnor Line Wagons Heavy Engine. Must run to time
No. 3 4, & 6 Must run to time. Through Trains to Cowes.
STAFF SECTION. Merstone Junction to Whitwell. Whitwell to Ventnor Town
N.B.—Every effort must be made to work the Branch Trains to time,
so that delay may not result to the Main Line Trains.

JULY to SEPTEMBER 1939

WEEKDAYS S.O. SUNDAYS

	a.m.	a.m.	a.m.	a.m.	p.m.	p.m.	p.m.	p.m.	p.m.	p.m.	p.m.	a.m.	p.m.	p.m.
Merstone	7.40	9.12	10.35	11.25	12.25	1.25	2.25	4.25	5.25	7.30	8.30	9.25	9.52 1.51	9.9
Godshill Halt	7.44	9.16	10.38	11.29	12.29	1.29	2.29	4.29	5.29	7.34	8.34	9.29	9.57 1.56	9.14
Whitwell	7.51	9.23	10.44	11.36	12.36	1.36	2.36	4.36	5.36	7.41	8.41	9.36	10.4 2.3	9.21
St. Lawrence Halt	7.57	9.29	10.48	11.42	12.42	1.42	2.42	4.42	5.42	7.47	8.47	9.42	10.9 2.8	9.26
Ventnor West	8.2	9.34	10.53	11.47	12.47	1.47	2.47	4.47	5.47	7.52	8.52	9.47	10.14 2.13	9.31

S.O. Saturdays only

WEEKDAYS S.O. SUNDAYS

	a.m.	a.m.	a.m.	a.m.	p.m.	p.m.	p.m.	p.m.	p.m.	p.m.	p.m.	a.m.	p.m.	p.m.
Ventnor West	8.15	9.40	10.58	11.55	12.55	1.55	2.55	4.55	6.20	7.8	8.58	9.58	10.28 2.30	9.36
St. Lawrence Halt	8.19	9.44	11. 2	11.59	12.59	1.59	2.59	4.59	6.24	8.2	9.2	10.2	10.32 2.34	9.40
Whitwell	8.24	9.49	11.7	12.4	1.4	2.4	3.4	5.4	6.29	8.7	9.7	10.7	10.37 2.39	9.46
Godshill Halt	8.31	9.56	11.13	12.11	1. 11	2.11	3.11	5.11	6.36	8.14	9.14	10.15	10.44 2.46	9.53
Merstone	8.36	10. 1	11.20	12.16	1. 16	2.16	3.16	5.16	6.41	8.19	9.19	10.20	10.49 2.51	9.58

S.O. Saturdays only

Tickets from the G.R.Croughton Collection

Closure

The early 1950's brought many closures to remote country branch lines where, a local bus service was considered adequate to cover the villages and small towns served by the particular line concerned. The Ventnor West branch fell into this category and although the line from Merstone to Ventnor was considered by many to be of unrivalled scenery, the fact remained that public use had progressively dwindled over a period of several years.

The Railway Executive of British Railways Southern Region announced that the branch would close on and from Monday September 15th 1952 due to "the policy of closing unrenumerative branch lines where adequate alternative services exist".

As there was no Sunday service, many local residents and railway enthusiasts made up the large crowd of people who waited at Merstone Junction for the last round trip over the branch on Saturday September 13th 1952. The two coach pull-and-push set (No.503) was pulled by 02 class 0-4-4T No. W 27 appropriately named "Merstone", the crew comprising of driver Jackie Sewell, fireman L. Harris and guard Reg Seaman. The engine sported small white boards on the front and the rear with the inscription "B. R. Farewell to Ventnor West 1900-1952".

In the fading light, the packed train pulled out of Merstone Junction for the very last time and was cheered by among others a group of Girl Guides who were camped quite near the line. At Godshill and Whitwell many more people gave the train a cheer before it entered the tunnel and then emerged to give the passengers a glorious view of the sea which was somewhat sombre in the dusk of the September evening. A stop at St. Lawrence and then along the leafy Undercliff to the terminus where, as the train arrived, a mighty cheer went up and fireworks were let off and streamers were thrown by the large crowd who had been gathering for some time, many having marched from the town behind the Ventnor Jazz Band lead by drum-major Jim White. There had been such a rush for tickets at the station (no doubt to be kept as souvenirs) that Alec Widger the booking clerk soon ran out of printed versions and was kept busy filling in blank tickets by hand. Some people even finished up with former Southern Railway tickets.

O2 class 0-4-4T No.W 27 "Merstone" with the branch train at Whitwell on September 13th 1952, the last day of public service.   Pamlin Prints

While the engine shunted and took on water, the jazz band marched up and down on the spare track. A BBC television cameraman was there also to record the last scene and although it seemed that there were far too many people waiting to travel than the two coach train could possibly take, somehow they all managed to squeeze in.

The guard's seven year old son Michael Seaman was given the honour of waving the green flag for the very last time and with the jazz band playing 'auld lang syne' the train pulled out just a few minutes after 8 p.m. to the sound of detonators which had been placed on the line.

Among those who saw the train off at Ventnor West was the Chairman of Ventnor Urban District Council Mr.S.A.Smith, the Deputy Assistant for the Islands railways Mr.A.L.Wallace and the Ventnor West stationmaster Mr.Harms. Three interested passengers on this the final journey were Mr.F.W.Channing, Mr.A.Norris and Mr.R.Hunt who were all former railwaymen who had in fact travelled on the very first train on the line. One other very interested passenger was Mr.G.Thorne from Rookley, who as a schoolboy saw the first sod of earth turned by Miss Beatrice Kate Martin at Merstone in April 1893.

Crowds of people waited at St. Lawrence, Whitwell and Godshill to give the train a final farewell. At Whitwell, cups of tea were served to the train crew by Mr.A.Western who lived in the station house and at Godshill someone pulled the communication cord just to add to the confusion. When the train arrived at Merstone it was greeted with more detonator sounds and, after the passengers had bid farewell to the train's crew, they watched as the train was then shunted into a siding. Any passengers who wanted to return to Ventnor would now have to either catch a bus or wait for a train to Sandown and then reach Ventnor at the former Isle of Wight Railway station which from then on became Ventnor's only station.

Ironically, although the former Isle of Wight Railway station once again became the only station at Ventnor when the 'West' station closed, it too closed in 1966 when the line from Ryde was cut back to Shanklin leaving Ventnor off the railway map completely.

O2 class 0-4-4T No.W 27 "Merstone" takes water at Ventnor West while pull-and-push set No.503 waits at the platform. September 13th 1952.   Pamlin Prints

27

O2 class 0-4-4T No.W 27 "Merstone" preparing to run round pull-and-push set No.503 at the buffer stops at Ventnor West Station on September 13th 1952. Pamlin Prints

O2 class 0-4-4T No.W 27 "Merstone" poses by the water column at Ventnor West. Surprisingly, No.W 27 was not fitted for pull-and-push working and was no doubt chosen for its name "Merstone". September 13th 1952. Pamlin Prints

28

The Present Scene

Although the branch to Ventnor West closed in 1952, the station at Merstone was still open as a through station on the Newport to Sandown route until that line finally closed on February 6th 1956.

At the time of writing, the only visible remains at Merstone is the very overgrown island platform, while the station building and the signal box have long since been demolished. Part of the site is now used as a car park. Gone are the days when the junction at Merstone was a great social centre where waiting passengers would chat between connections for Ventnor West, Sandown or Newport.

Very little remains to be seen of the former route of the line, although the station buildings at all four branch stations (which were always considered to be some of the best on the Island) still remain and are now in the hands of private owners.

In 1984, the northern end of the St. Lawrence Tunnel was opened as the Whitwell Mushroom Farm with access gained along the former trackbed from Dean Crossing.

The stone built former station building at Ventnor West is now surrounded by modern bungalows and what was once the trackbed is now a road. As you walk along this road, it is hard to believe that this area was once a station. What would Mr.Percy Mortimer and his brother Charles (who negotiated so long and hard for the site) say if they stood at the former terminus today.

The former platform at Merstone where the trackbed is now a car park. June 2005.
Nick Catford

The station site at Merstone before demolition. May 21st 1960.
G.R.Croughton

Two views of the former Godshill Station. *(Left)* Looking towards Whitwell in June 1977. *(Right)* Looking towards Merstone in June 1975.   Nick Catford

This June 2005 view of the former station at Whitwell shows that not a great deal appears to have changed apart from filling in between the platforms and adding gates and a phone box.   Nick Catford

(Left) The north portal of the St. Lawrence Tunnel in June 2005. For some years this end of the tunnel was used as a mushroom farm. *(Right)* The south portal of the tunnel also in June 2005.   Nick Catford

Conclusion

Like so many similar lines which set out with such high hopes for the future, the Ventnor West railway simply became a country branch line serving a remote part of the Island. If the line had reached closer to the town of Ventnor and if the optimistic hopes of through traffic from the mainland via Southampton and Cowes had developed into a reality instead of a promise, the line might have stood a better chance. If the Solent Tunnel (which would have connected Lymington and Yarmouth) had been built, the branch might have stood an even better chance, but, this was not to be.

Looking back in time, one wonders what would Mr.T.D.Bolton M.P., the Chairman of the Isle of Wight Central Railway in 1897 say today if he saw what had happened to the Islands railways. Remember, that when the branch was first opened to St. Lawrence in 1897, he made the following statement "It was his honest belief that the Isle of Wight owed its prosperity to the railways and to nothing else. Might they flourish root and branch till time and memory be no more".

Both platforms at Ventnor West. August 18th 1938. R.F.Roberts

Happy memories at Ventnor West as O2 class 0-4-4T No.W 35 "Freshwater" approaches the platform.
Lens of Sutton

Acknowledgements

Many thanks to the following people and organisations for their kind help in compiling information and supplying photographs for both the original and revised publication:
John Scott-Morgan, Mr.G.R.Croughton, Pamlin Prints, Mr.J.J.Smith, Miss A. Russell, The L.C.G.B. for the Ken Nunn Collection, Mrs.D.Cooke, Mr.J.M.Fisher, Mr.R.Stumpf, Isle of Wight County Press and the Public Records Office at Kew.

I would like place on record the help and encouragement I have received over many years from the following gentlemen who have supplied photographs and information and who are now unfortunately no longer with us:- Mr.R.C.Riley, Mr.S.W.Baker, Mr.D.Cullum, Mr.R.F.Roberts, Mr.J.L.Smith (of Lens of Sutton) and Mr.H.C.Casserley.

My thanks as always to Norman Branch for reading my text and to James Christian of Binfield Printers Limited for his help.

Bibliography

THE ISLE OF WIGHT CENTRAL RAILWAY by R.J.Maycock and R.Silsbury (Oakwood Press)
THE ISLE OF WIGHT RAILWAYS by Michael Robbins (Oakwood Press)
A LOCOMOTIVE HISTORY OF RAILWAYS ON THE ISLE OF WIGHT by D.L. Bradley (The Railway Correspondence and Travel Society)
SOUTHERN RAILWAY BRANCH LINE TRAINS by RW.Kidner (Oakwood Press)
RAILS IN THE ISLE OF WIGHT by P.C.Allen and A.B. MacLeod (David & Charles)
STEAMING THROUGH THE ISLE OF WIGHT by Peter Hay (Middleton Press)
ONCE UPON A LINE Vol. 1 & 2 by Andrew Britton (Oxford Publishing)
ISLE OF WIGHT RAILWAYS REMEMBERED by Peter Paye (Oxford Publishing)
BRANCH LINES TO NEWPORT by Vic Mitchell and Keith Smith (Middleton Press)
WIGHT REPORT (Various issues)
RAILWAY MAGAZINE (Various issues)
RAILWAY WORLD (Various issues)

The former Ventnor West Station. October 26th 1986. *Author*